W9-AMP-312

"Fat Man," the atomic bomb dropped on Nagasaki.

Atom Bomb

Six miles in the sky was no place to run out of gas! This was just the latest in a series of problems that Major Charles Sweeney, aircraft commander of the B-29 Superfortress, V-77, named *Bock's Car*, had had to deal with. Almost eight hours earlier, at 3:47 A.M., August 9, 1945, Sweeney and a 12-man crew had taken off from an airstrip on Tinian in the Mariana Islands. They had flown northwest across the Pacific Ocean all morning, aiming for Kyushu, southernmost of the Japanese islands. Now they might not have enough gas to get back to a safe base.

A Japanese soldier searches in the rubble for anything worth salvaging.

Back in the bomb bay, a pumpkin-colored monster atomic bomb, combat unit F31, nicknamed "Fat Man," strained against its shackles. Sweeney believed his mission could end World War II—if he could find a target!

Three B-29's were in Special Bombing Mission No. 16. *Bock's Car*, named after its usual pilot, Captain Frederick Bock, would drop the bomb. Captain Bock was flying Major Sweeney's regular plane, *The Great Artiste*.

Atom Bomb

Tom Seddon

Scientific
BOOKS FOR YOUNG READERS
American

W.H. Freeman and Company
New York

SHENENDEHOWA PUBLIC LIBRARY
47 CLIFTON COUNTRY ROAD
CLIFTON PARK, NEW YORK 12065
114903

Scientists in *The Great Artiste* planned to drop special pressure gauges, nicknamed Bangmeters, to measure the blast of "Fat Man." The plane also carried an official journalist, reporter William Laurence of *The New York Times.* The third B-29, *Full House*, flown by Major James Hopkins, carried more observers, equipped with a variety of cameras.

The problems had started before they left the ground. At least a day before, the crew assembling "Fat Man" discovered that the bolt holes in the front section of the bomb's armor-plated case did not line up with the holes in the rear section. The crew tried to adjust the case, but nothing worked. They decided instead to use a bomb case of thin steel used for practice bomb drops. This jacket fit perfectly. But if bullets or a piece of shrapnel struck this thin case, the bomb might be destroyed before it could explode.

For good luck, the entire bomb assembly crew, fifty people or more, wrote their names and rude slogans on the finished bomb. The completed bomb was loaded into the front bomb bay of *Bock's Car* without further problems.

Then, just before takeoff, flight engineer Sergeant John "Nails" Kuharek discovered he could not transfer reserve fuel from the tank in the rear bomb bay. Six hundred gallons of extra fuel was just extra weight.

Three hours into the flight came a real scare. The "black box" device that monitored the bomb's circuits suddenly began to flash wildly out of control. Ten frantic minutes raced by as the box was dismantled. Finally, two switches were discovered to have been set backward, and they were reset. The red light resumed its steady flashing. All was well. No one had any idea why it had taken hours for the box to start acting funny.

Bock's Car's target was the weapons arsenal at Kokura, Japan. But when *Bock's Car* arrived, Kokura was shrouded in a heavy smoke and haze. For 45 minutes, Sweeney's crew searched for their aiming point. Meanwhile, Japanese pilots were rising to attack, and anti-aircraft artillery exploded flak near *Bock's Car*. Sweeney had no choice but to turn his bomber toward the second-choice target.

The shadows of a Japanese soldier, killed instantly in the explosion, and a ladder were printed on a wall.

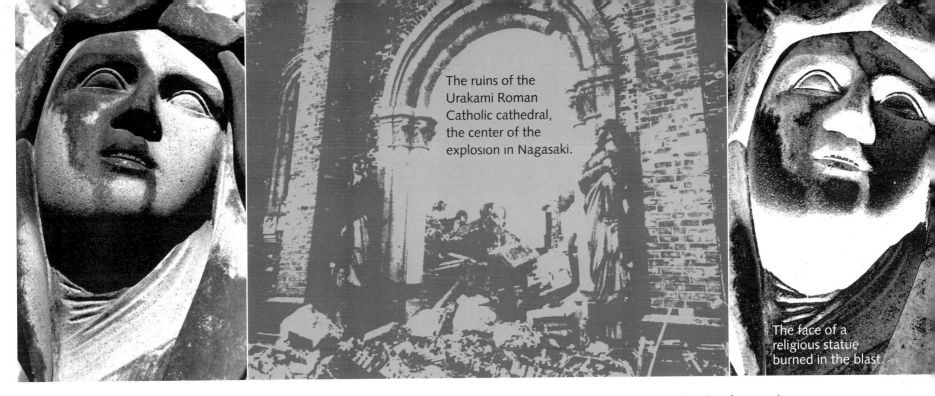

The ruins of the Urakami Roman Catholic cathedral, the center of the explosion in Nagasaki.

The face of a religious statue burned in the blast.

He cursed his luck when he found that it, too, was under thickening cloud cover. Sweeney had orders for visual bombing only—no radar—but the fuel situation was critical. He asked atomic weaponeer Navy Lieutenant Commander Frederick Ashworth to agree to drop the bomb using the strictly forbidden radar.

"We'll let it go over Nagasaki," Ashworth said after a long pause. "Visually, radar, or what have you."

Soon, Bombardier Captain Kermit Beahan was crouched over the telescopic eyepiece of the bombsight in the Plexiglas nose of the aircraft. As he guided *Bock's Car* over a fortunate hole in the clouds, Beahan spotted a stadium near the giant Mitsubishi arms manufacturing plant. This factory had made the torpedoes used in the Japanese attack on American ships at Pearl Harbor in Hawaii—which dragged the United States into World War II.

Quickly, Beahan locked the bomb release. The bombsight flew the plane automatically. Seconds later the ingenious electromechanical computer cut the massive bomb loose.

"Bombs away!" Beahan yelled, as *Bock's Car*, several tons lighter, lurched up into the air.

The historic city of Nagasaki was bustling about its routine Thursday morning business. Its citizens were totally unaware that a horrible death was being delivered.

1

Becquerel's Rays Lead to Frisch's Fission

Henri Becquerel

With a brilliant flash of eerie greenish-white light, "Fat Man" signaled the end of World War II. The raging fireball rising over Nagasaki, like the one over Hiroshima three days earlier, marked the troubled dawn of the atomic age.

The bombs that exploded over the two Japanese cities were not normal high explosives generated by ordinary chemical reactions. Their fantastic power came instead from the mighty forces that weld together the atom—the building block of all chemical elements.

Atomic bombs are more properly called nuclear weapons, because their explosive energy once glued together tiny particles that make up the core of the atom, the nucleus. Splitting—fissioning—the nucleus releases the pent-up energy. To cause a nuclear explosion one has to trigger an uncontrolled "chain reaction" of splitting atoms.

Chemical elements that fission are rare. However, each gives off special kinds of energetic rays, or radiation. Such elements are termed radioactive. A half-century before *Bock's Car* flew into the history books, scientists curious about the puzzle of radioactivity had begun probing the atom's secrets.

Paris, France, 1896

X rays, recently discovered, caused fluorescent minerals to glow in the dark. Physicist Henri Becquerel wondered: If exposure to X rays made fluorescent minerals glow, did glowing fluorescent minerals give off X rays?

Following up earlier tests, Becquerel sealed several photographic plates in light-tight aluminum holders and put them, with minerals on top, inside a dark drawer. Growing impatient while waiting for a sunny day to start the fluorescence, he went ahead and developed the plates anyway. To his immense surprise, "shadows" of the specimens appeared "with great intensity!" Becquerel immediately knew he had hit upon something brand-new. The images on his plates were not caused by fluorescence or by X rays.

Becquerel soon learned that the key ingredients of the minerals he used were uranium compounds. In fact, pure uranium metal worked best.

Becquerel's friend and fellow physicist in Paris, Pierre Curie, together with his Polish-born wife, Marie Sklodowska Curie, soon began a lifelong study of the mysterious, penetrating "Becquerel rays," which they named radioactivity. The Curies isolated new radioactive elements— polonium and radium—from uranium ore. Marie Curie won Nobel prizes in both physics and chemistry for her trailblazing work.

Over the next 30 years, experimenters slowly discovered more secrets of the atom.

Pierre and Marie Curie

Ernest Rutherford

1897–1920

Natural radioactivity was sorted into three types, called (for convenience) alpha, beta, and gamma, after the first three letters of the Greek alphabet. The negatively charged electron was discovered. New Zealander Ernest Rutherford found that an atom has a massive core—which was named the nucleus. Protons, with their positive electric charge, were located there.

1932

James Chadwick

James Chadwick discovered the neutron in the nucleus. The neutron has the same mass as a proton but has no electric charge. Neutrons explained the existence of isotopes—atoms that are chemically identical but vary in weight because they have different numbers of neutrons in their nuclei. Different isotopes are chemically identical but radioactively quite different.

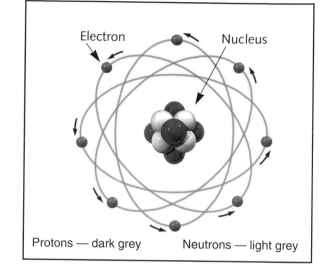

Electron   Nucleus

Protons — dark grey   Neutrons — light grey

1934

The Curies' daughter, Irène, along with her husband, Frédéric Joliot, caused a sensation! They made ordinary aluminum radioactive by blasting it with alpha radiation.

Inspired, the young physicist Enrico Fermi and his friends at the University of Rome went one step further. They used neutrons to bombard every element that they could obtain. Out of about sixty elements, more than forty became radioactive.

The heaviest of these was uranium, element 92. By bombarding uranium with neutrons, Fermi's group hoped to create an element never found in nature, element 93. (Actually, without realizing it, they also, by chance, produced the first nuclear fissions.)

German chemist Ida Noddack suggested that being struck by neutrons might cause a uranium nucleus to break into several large radioactive chunks. Her theory was the first suggestion that the nucleus of an atom might fission. Her idea was called "really absurd"; Noddack was ignored.

Irène and
Frédéric Joliot-Curie

Enrico Fermi

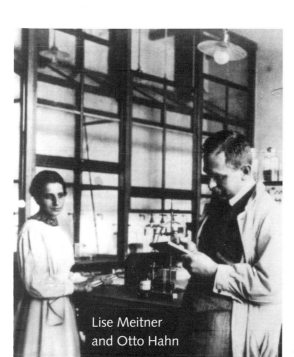

Lise Meitner
and Otto Hahn

Otto Frisch

Adolf Hitler

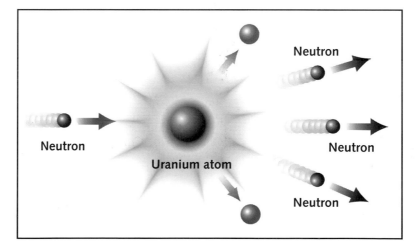

1938

At the Kaiser Wilhelm Institute in Berlin, a German chemist, Otto Hahn, and an Austrian nuclear physicist, Lise Meitner, had been studying radioactive elements for more than twenty years. Meitner, a Jew, had to flee Germany. Chancellor Adolf Hitler had started his savage torture, imprisonment, and destruction of European Jews.

Hahn forged ahead with another partner, chemist Fritz Strassmann. They concluded that a seemingly new isotope they had isolated was actually radioactive barium. But barium was element number 56. How could uranium, element 92, change into barium, element 56? In December, Hahn wrote to Lise Meitner, safe in Stockholm, Sweden, about their curious results.

Meitner, together with her nephew Otto Frisch, who lived in nearby Copenhagen, Denmark, worked out what must have happened in Hahn and Strassman's experiments. They boldly declared that the uranium atom had been burst apart by the neutrons. Ida Noddack had been right after all!

Shortly after his return to Copenhagen, Frisch hurried to tell the famous physicist Niels Bohr about this remarkable finding. Bohr, who was about to leave for a trip to the United States, struck his head and said, "Oh, what fools we have been! We ought to have seen that before."

Neutron

Neutron

Neutron

Neutron

Uranium atom

9

Niels
Bohr

January 26, 1939

At the Fifth Annual Washington Conference on Theoretical Physics, Bohr announced the discovery of fission to a large group of American physicists. A few days later, the team of Frédéric and Irène Joliot-Curie and Yugoslavian Paul Savitch published their own results: "Experimental proof of the explosive rupture of the uranium nucleus. . . ."

Scientists around the world were excited by the news. They rushed to their laboratories to see if they, too, could make uranium atoms fission. Soon physicists in many countries were blasting neutrons at uranium. In 1939 alone, more than one hundred scientific papers were published on atomic fission.

April 30, 1939

These two headlines ran in *The New York Times*::

BRITAIN PREPARES FOR A CRISIS—
AS HITLER THREATENS POLAND

VISION EARTH ROCKED
BY ISOTOPE BLAST
Scientists Say Bit of Uranium
Could Wreck New York

Another headline announced the opening of the New York World's Fair, with its theme "The World of Tomorrow."

A grim tomorrow seemed to be in the making. Nuclear scientists recognized from the start that uranium fission was a potential source of great power. If billions of atoms fissioned in a chain reaction, powerful bombs were possible. The first country to figure out how to make atomic fission bombs would win the European war that looked unavoidable.

2

Professor Einstein Writes a Letter

Leo Szilard

Early 1939

It is one thing to produce a few isolated fissions, but quite another actually to build a fission bomb. There were many questions without answers.

Which isotopes of what elements could be made to fission?
How could the isotopes that fissioned be isolated?
What type of fission fragments are formed?
How much energy is released?
Does one fission release extra neutrons?
If so, how many extra neutrons are released?
Is it possible to start a chain of fission reactions, with each triggering more fissions?

Leo Szilard, a Hungarian physicist, felt that finding answers to these questions was urgent. Convinced that Hitler in Germany and Mussolini in Italy would bring the world to war, he fled Europe to join Enrico Fermi at Columbia University. After winning the Nobel Prize for physics in 1938, Fermi had become alarmed by Italy's fascist government. He feared for the safety of his Jewish wife. Szilard, Fermi, and other immigrant scientists were terrified by the thought of Germany making an atomic bomb.

The key was whether each fission released "stray" neutrons, which could trigger more fissions. Deciding to tackle the research himself, Szilard worked with Dr. Walter Zinn at Columbia. On the evening of March 3, Szilard telephoned Edward Teller, a friend from Hungary now at George Washington University in Washington, D.C. Speaking excitedly in Hungarian, Szilard said, "I have found the neutrons."

Herbert Anderson

Albert Einstein

President Franklin D. Roosevelt

Over the next few months Szilard, Fermi, and fellow scientist Herbert Anderson experimented on uranium fission. They seemed to be on the right track toward a chain reaction of fissioning atoms.

Because Szilard felt that this research must be kept secret from the Germans, he tried to get nuclear physicists to stop sending reports on their discoveries to scientific journals. He had little success.

Even more important, President Franklin D. Roosevelt had to be spurred into action. Desperate, Szilard called on an old friend—Albert Einstein, who at age 60 was the most famous scientist in the world. Perhaps Roosevelt would listen to Einstein. Szilard talked him into signing a letter he would write. But how could they be sure the President would read it?

Events took a promising turn when Szilard was introduced to Dr. Alexander Sachs, who knew President Roosevelt personally. Sachs promised to place the letter from Einstein in Roosevelt's hands but said he'd have to wait for the right moment.

September 1, 1939

Hitler's armies invaded Poland. On September 3, England and France declared war on Germany. Roosevelt was busy trying to find ways to help England.

Finally, on October 11, Sachs had a private meeting with Roosevelt. Presenting Einstein's letter, he spoke of nuclear power production, the medical uses of radioactivity, and the possibility of powerful bombs.

The President responded by creating an Advisory Committee on Uranium and naming Dr. Lyman Briggs, director of Washington's Bureau of Standards, as chairman. The committee would supervise uranium research, providing money for expenses.

Both the Army and the Navy were represented on the committee. The military was skeptical of scientific gizmos. But when Teller asked for six thousand dollars to support Fermi's chain reaction experiments, the request was granted. This was the first of the two *billion* dollars that the U. S. government would spend on the atomic bomb project over the next six years.

3

The Heat Is On

December 1941

Two eventful years had passed since President Roosevelt established the original Advisory Committee on Uranium. Many scientists were alarmed at the slow pace of the bomb research. Hitler's armies were conquering Europe. Poland, Denmark, Norway, Holland, Belgium, and France had fallen in turn. Bomber attacks on England had begun in August 1940. And in the summer of 1941, Hitler's army struck at Russia. For freedom's sake, the United States had to build the bomb first!

In late fall 1941, research with military applications was centralized in the new Office of Scientific Research and Development headed by Vannevar Bush. By then, 16 projects on uranium fission research had spent $300,000.

In 1940, Edwin McMillan and Philip Abelson had achieved Fermi's dream of making a new element, number 93. A few months later Glenn Seaborg, Arthur Wahl, and Joseph Kennedy created element 94. Element 93 was named neptunium, and element 94 was called plutonium. Experiments were now undertaken to try to fission plutonium from the tiny amounts produced in atom-smashing machines.

On December 7, 1941, Japanese bombers attacked the U.S. naval base of Pearl Harbor, near Honolulu, Hawaii. The next day the United States declared war on Japan, which was already at war with China. Germany declared war on the United States. Allies of the United States joined the fight. Almost the whole world was now at war.

Nine days later, a meeting was held to review progress toward a working atomic bomb. Bush, suggesting that the Army take over the entire project, began to transfer all major building projects to the Army Corps of Engineers. Colonel James Marshall was named head of a new district created solely to produce the bomb. Since Marshall's headquarters were in New York City, he called his "cover" for the bomb work the Manhattan Engineer District. The Manhattan Project—the name by which the bomb research would be known—was born.

General Leslie Groves

September 1942

The project stumbled along. Bush quietly pushed for stronger leadership. His choice: Colonel Leslie Groves. Admired as a strong, aggressive leader, this career Army man was a trained engineer whose latest project had been the Pentagon building. Groves was not pleased to be chosen. But the Army approved of Bush's choice. Eager to accept a combat engineering position in the European war, he was now stuck in the United States building factories and supervising scientists. To ease the sting, the Army promoted him to brigadier general.

Groves got right to work. Within a week he broke through many of the roadblocks that had stalled the program. He bought a huge supply of uranium ore that had been sitting in a warehouse. He started the paperwork to purchase 59,000 acres (24,000 hectares) of land along the Clinch River in northeastern Tennessee, near Knoxville. This was "Site X," code named the "Clinton Engineer Works," the place to build industrial factories plants to process uranium for use in an atomic bomb.

Shortly afterward, Groves set out to tour all Manhattan Engineer District labs. He had been assured that the scientific research was nearly complete. Transferred to the University of Chicago, Szilard and Fermi had been working toward a continuous chain reaction. They built larger and larger "nuclear" piles of uranium slugs inside carbon bricks. Groves asked the scientists to estimate as closely as possible how much fissionable material the bomb needed—its "critical mass." He was shocked to find out that the estimate was little better than a guess. Why was this so?

A major problem had come up with uranium. Only the isotope of uranium called uranium-235 (U^{235})—with 92 protons and 143 neutrons in its nucleus—fissions easily and could be the fuel for a nuclear chain reaction. But only 7 of every 1,000 atoms of natural uranium have this combination. The rest are U^{238}, with 92 protons and 146 neutrons.

Imagine sorting through a pile of 1,000 bowling balls, trying to find 7 that are just 3 ounces (90 grams) lighter than all the rest. What sort of scale could be used to weigh atoms? How do you build an atom sifter? No one had ever separated the different isotopes of an element in more than tiny amounts.

Site X

Ernest Lawrence with the machine he created to separate U^{235} atoms from U^{238} atoms.

The electromagnetic separation racetrack at Site X.

At the same time, Fermi and other scientists working on uranium fission hoped that they could use plutonium instead. If so, a bomb might be made from plutonium. But no one knew enough about plutonium to be sure how to produce it in quantity—or even whether it would fission. So far they had produced only a few millionths of a gram of plutonium. Intense neutron bombardment inside a nuclear pile was thought capable of converting—"transmuting"—some uranium into plutonium, but no one knew how to do that either. General Groves watched impatiently as the scientists debated endlessly.

What was Groves to do? During his visit to the Radiation Laboratory of the University of California at Berkeley, California, Nobel Prize–winner Dr. Ernest Lawrence had enthusiastically pushed "electromagnetic separation" as the way to separate the isotopes of uranium. A particle accelerator shot charged uranium atoms into a vacuum between the poles of a powerful magnet that resembled a huge waffle iron 15 feet (4.5 meters) across. This strong magnetic field bent the charged particles into a circular arc, with the lighter particles bending more sharply than the heavier ones. The separate stream of U^{235} atoms could be collected in a tiny "bucket."

Groves ordered a production plant built for the electromagnetic separation method of extracting U^{235}. He ordered giant plants for other methods, called gaseous and thermal diffusion. These methods relied on the lighter U^{235} atoms being "speedier" than the more "sluggish" U^{238} atoms. Finally, he ordered Fermi's group to come up with the design for a plutonium production nuclear reactor. Groves was gambling millions of dollars, and he knew it.

4

The First Reactor

December 2, 1942

"Pull it to thirteen feet, George," ordered physicist Enrico Fermi from the balcony of the squash court in the University of Chicago football stadium. George Weil carefully slid the cadmium-plated wooden rod backward.

The squash court wasn't heated, but the scientists crowded on the balcony weren't shuffling around to keep warm.

The Chicago group of physicists, chemists, and engineers had been code-named the Metallurgical Laboratory, "Met Lab" for short. Months of hard work at Met Lab had led to this exciting day. If this experiment failed, it was likely that the whole atomic bomb project would fail.

As the control rod moved back, the idle ticking of radiation counters became a rapid click-clack. Weil stopped when 13 feet (4 meters) of rod stayed buried in the hulk next to him. The chart recorder pen shot upward, along with the tension in the room.

"The trace will go to this point and level off," Fermi announced, pointing to the graph. Sure enough, it did.

The "Met Lab" scientists at their fourth anniversary reunion.

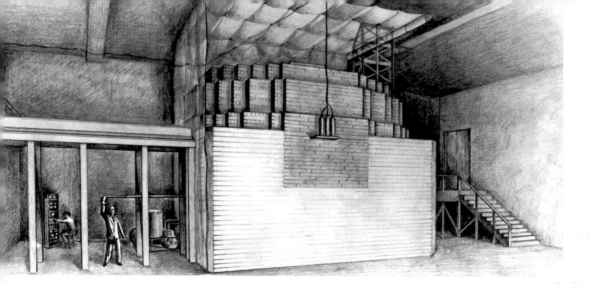

Chicago Pile Number One

Fermi and his lab bosses were huddled around the main instrument rack. Down on the floor of the squash court a massive frame of wooden timbers stood 14 feet (4.3 meters) tall. What was this huge structure?

Fermi had calculated he'd need 100,000 pounds (45,000 kilograms) of natural uranium to start a U^{235} fission chain reaction that could keep itself going. Since U^{238} atoms soaked up fast neutrons like a sponge (the first step in making plutonium), the uranium "slugs" were spaced apart in holes in carbon blocks. The carbon atoms slowed down the neutrons, so the U^{235} atoms fissioned freely.

Workers, stripped to the waist, their skin glistening black from carbon dust, stacked layer upon layer of carbon bricks into a rough mound supported by wooden timbers. Almost sixty layers, up to 24 feet (7.4 meters) across—40,000 bricks—were needed. Above the wooden frame walls, the top layers were formed into a crude mound. This was the first nuclear reactor, called simply Chicago Pile Number One.

Now, under watchful eyes, the control rod was slowly pulled out, causing more and more of the U^{235} atoms within the pile to fission. If the reactions ever surged out of control, it could be disastrous. The carefully tended heat from the nuclear furnace might become a raging inferno. The control rod under Weil's care was absorbing the extra neutrons freed by fission. It was the damper that choked back the nuclear "fire."

All at once, a clang as loud as a thunderclap froze everybody in place. Was the nuclear reaction out of control? Would the pile melt down? Would it explode?

For a moment, the room was deathly still. Even the neutron counters were quiet.

There was no emergency. An automatic safety rod had clapped into the pile. Apparently the safety switch had been preset too low. The reactor had turned itself off. With a big smile, Fermi looked around and said, "I'm hungry. Let's go to lunch."

After lunch, the experiment continued. The pile was swarming with neutrons, free now to rush anywhere in the pile. Countless fissions were being triggered in the U^{235} atoms, which in turn triggered countless more.

By 3:25 p.m., the reaction was self-sustaining. For the next 28 minutes the group quietly watched the world's first nuclear reactor. Leona Woods, the one woman in the group, remembered looking around and suspecting that, like her, everyone else was thinking ahead to the atomic bomb.

By early 1943, bulldozers were at work at Oak Ridge—Site X—in Tennessee. Some of the largest industrial buildings in the world were built by a construction crew that peaked at 47,000 workers. One mammoth U-shaped building alone was wider than a football field. Each leg of the U was nearly half a mile long.

By 1945, three production plants for U^{235} were operating as stages of one continuous process. The output of the thermal diffusion plant was fed into the gaseous diffusion plant. This product was fed into the electromagnetic machines, named calutrons, for the final separation.

There were plenty of bugs in the system, but each difficulty was eventually overcome. It took until March 1944 to begin delivering U^{235}. A year later the plants were cranking it out.

By July 24, 1945, enough 90-percent-pure U^{235} had been generated to make one atomic bomb.

An aerial view of the Oak Ridge plant.

5

Don't Harm the Salmon

The isolated and guarded Hanford Engineer Works.

1943–1944

Plutonium did fission! Separating plutonium from uranium looked to be easier than sifting out U^{235} atoms.

For the production of plutonium, Oak Ridge would not have enough room. As many as six nuclear reactors and three plutonium-separation plants might be needed, so General Groves sent his staff looking for more land.

Their search of major western rivers with hydroelectric power plants led them to a desertlike area in southeastern Washington. They chose a spot on the west bank of the Columbia River, famous for its salmon. It was isolated and sparsely populated. It was near plenty of electric power and fresh, cold water to cool the reactors. Groves was given the go-ahead but was warned not to "harm a single scale on a single salmon."

As construction workers were recruited from all over the United States, the Hanford Engineer Works—an area more than half as large as the state of Rhode Island—ballooned to a huge camp of 45,000 residents. With miles of high barbed-wire fences and armed guards at the gates, it looked like a prison camp. Winters were freezing; summers were broiling. The camp was attacked by swarms of insects and hit by sandstorms. Getting a meal meant crowding into one of eight mess halls with four thousand other workers. Fights were common among the brawny men. The Hanford jail had room for 27 prisoners, which was often not enough.

The workers were baffled about what they were building. Secrecy was so complete that even the amount of ice cream eaten by the workers was classified. The job of the press relations officer was to suppress any genuine stories about the project. Keeping the crews totally in the dark made it hard to convince them that their work was vital to the war effort. Small wonder that morale was low.

September 1944

On September 13, Enrico Fermi had the honor of inserting the first uranium fuel slug into an "industrial-strength" nuclear reactor: Pile B at Hanford. If all went well, this giant would soon be cranking out plutonium for atomic bombs. Loading and testing took two weeks. Finally, minutes after midnight on September 27, the safety rods were withdrawn and the control rods were pulled out a bit. The fission chain reactions started. Pile B was over a million times more powerful than Chicago Pile Number One.

Spring 1945

By now, three nuclear reactors were operating. They were giant versions of the Chicago pile.

Since it takes tons of uranium to produce mere grams of plutonium, immense amounts of deadly radioactive waste products are left over. With the wartime emergency driving the Manhattan Project, the Hanford managers simply stored the liquid radioactive wastes in steel tanks. Fifty years later, the problem of how to dispose of them safely has not been solved.

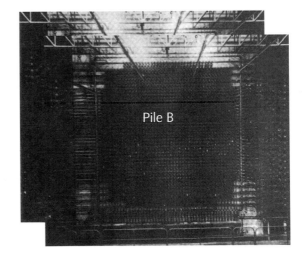

Pile B

6

Oppy's Ranch School

J. Robert
Oppenheimer

Worried about security, General Groves had tried to restrict the flow of bomb information between labs. This infuriated the scientists, who were used to stimulating discussions and free exchanges of information. Groves considered drafting all the scientists into the Army. J. Robert Oppenheimer had a different idea. "Oppy" was a theoretical physicist who had been brought into the bomb project a year earlier by Ernest Lawrence to check calculations on the size of the bomb. He was now to be the boss of an operation to make a working bomb. Oppenheimer suggested gathering the scientists together at an isolated lab. He knew of just the place, a remote mesa top in northern New Mexico.

Events moved quickly. On December 7, 1942, exactly one year after Pearl Harbor, at a special assembly, students at the Los Alamos Ranch School, near Santa Fe, New Mexico, were amazed to hear a letter from Secretary of War Henry Stimson. Their school was needed for the war effort. Christmas vacation was canceled. On January 21, 1943, the school closed its doors forever. By mid-April, construction crews were swarming over "Site Y."

Los Alamos Laboratory

Housing for four thousand civilians and two thousand military personnel was built. Bringing enough electric power, heating fuel, water, and telephone service to the remote mountain site was a constant headache. The buildings of the Tech Area were enclosed in stout fencing topped with barbed wire. Another fence ran around the entire town site. Military police in battle helmets secured the few gates. The perimeter fence was patrolled by mounted soldiers.

Unlike Oak Ridge and Hanford, Los Alamos was established as a maximum-security military reservation completely enclosing the civilian homes and scientific labs. Its very existence was top secret. Residents were forbidden to mention its name in letters, all of which were opened and read by Army censors.

An aerial view of Los Alamos, with its huge complex of buildings.

The four divisions of scientists at Los Alamos had their hands full. The Theoretical Division was trying mathematically to track the neutrons in a fissioning chain reaction. Based on theory, how much material would be needed for a critical mass? Calculations were slow, and computation machines built for banks by the International Business Machine Company (IBM) were bought to do the job.

Everyone knew that an atomic bomb would create temperatures of millions of degrees. One member of the group, Leo Szilard's friend Edward Teller, had startled the others by presenting calculations showing that it might ignite the entire atmosphere. But the group leader, Hans Bethe, proved that such a disaster was not very likely. Nonetheless, the remote chance of destroying the whole planet haunted the project.

While the Chemistry and Metallurgy Division concentrated on purifying uranium and plutonium samples that arrived from Oak Ridge and Hanford, the Experimental Physics Division had to work with the tiny amounts already available. They sought to know: How many neutrons were released from a single fission, and how quickly? How fast did they move, and how far did they have to travel before they caused another fission?

Most fissions released at least two neutrons. These two could each trigger another fission, releasing a total of at least four neutrons. By doubling in each "generation," a huge number of neutrons could be released in eighty to ninety steps—enough to flood a bomb-sized critical mass with fissioning atoms.

The group worked out details for the size and shape of the bomb. A melon-sized ball of pure U^{235} was expected to do the job. Because uranium is denser even than lead, the ball would weigh 123 pounds (about 56 kilograms). This was the critical mass for bare U^{235}. To use anything less would allow too many neutrons to escape from the surface without furthering the chain reaction.

The trick, then, was to start with two pieces, each one half of the critical mass. Neither half could explode by itself. But slamming the two halves together would trigger the fast chain reaction and the explosion. The two pieces must slam together fast, because the complete chain reaction would take less than a millionth of a second!

The scientists designed a simple atomic bomb: Shape one piece of U^{235} so that it can be screwed onto the end of a 6-foot (2-meter) piece of an artillery cannon barrel. From the other end, fire a large bullet of U^{235}. When the bullet smashes into the piece on the end, the resulting critical mass will instantly set off an atomic explosion. Easier said than done, of course!

The Ordnance Division set to work on this "gun barrel" method of assembling the two less-than-critical masses. Because of great concern that a chain reaction might be triggered prematurely, work was begun on another idea—implosion—that had been put forth by Richard Tolman and Robert Serber. A sub-critical mass would be blown inward by an outer layer of ordinary explosives.

When Los Alamos scientist Emilio Segrè proved that the "gun barrel" method would not work with plutonium, and after it was discovered that plutonium undergoes spontaneous fission, implosion research went full speed ahead. From a handful of scientists, led by Seth Neddermeyer, the implosion group grew to hundreds. One of the excellent theoretical physicists who worked on implosion was Klaus Fuchs.

Isidor Rabi

Robert Serber

Hans Bethe

Enrico Fermi

George Kistiakowsky

John Von Neumann

Victor Weisskopf

Edward Teller

Emilio Segrè

Richard Feynman

Seth Neddermeyer

27

7

Fuchs Steals the Secret

Klaus Fuchs

Winter–Summer 1944

Bundled up against the New York City cold, Klaus Fuchs must have felt a little foolish carrying a tennis ball. At a street corner on the Lower East Side, he spotted his contact. The tip-off was the second pair of gloves the man was carrying under his arm and a book with a distinctive green cover he was holding.

Fuchs knew him only as "Raymond"—his new courier to the Russians. Raymond was really Harry Gold, a chemist for a sugar refinery in Philadelphia. Gold was also smuggling American industrial secrets to the Soviet Union.

The Soviets were our allies, although many Americans distrusted them and their communist government. In any event, passing U.S. government secrets, even to an ally, was spying!

During the next few months, Fuchs and Gold met several more times. Fuchs handed over bundles of pages of handwritten notes. Then, one summer day, Fuchs failed to show up. Where had he gone? To Los Alamos, to work on the bomb.

German-born Klaus Fuchs, a theoretical physicist, was a refugee from Nazi tyranny. While living in England, Fuchs had seemed to be nothing more than a brilliant scientist. But like many other intellectuals of his day, he believed only communism could defeat facism. What did Fuchs tell the Soviets? Everything he knew or could find out.

Soon after his arrival in New York, he had leaked detailed designs of the gaseous diffusion plant at Oak Ridge. Now he was at Los Alamos. What did he give away while there? He gave away the store!

June 1945

At first, military intelligence people had routinely tailed the Los Alamos scientists and their families on their one-day-per-month holiday in Santa Fe. But on this Saturday afternoon, no one was following Klaus Fuchs's Buick. At 4:00 P.M., on the Castillo Bridge, he picked up his old contact from New York, Harry Gold. He handed over more than a hundred pages of detailed notes on the bomb.

Gold's next stop was an apartment in Albuquerque where Los Alamos machinist David Greenglass was visiting his wife. Gold recited his coded identification: "I bear greetings from Julius." He showed Greenglass half of a Jell-O boxtop cut in a zigzag pattern. Greenglass pulled the matching half from his wife's purse. Identification was confirmed.

Greenglass was also the brother of Ethel Rosenberg—who, along with her husband, Julius, would be convicted in 1951 of actively spying for the Soviet Union and executed two years later. Greenglass helped machine the molds for the high-explosive parts of the implosion design. He also kept his ears open. Greenglass had a long talk with Gold and made some sketches of his work.

On the train back to New York, Gold carried the news that the new plutonium implosion design was going to be tested. Within a month, Los Alamos scientists would attempt to detonate the first nuclear explosion.

Ethel and Julius Rosenberg

8

The Test

Monday, July 16, 1945

The world's first nuclear detonation, a test of the plutonium implosion design, was scheduled for 4:00 A.M. at a place Oppenheimer had code-named Trinity site. It was 160 miles (260 kilometers) south of Los Alamos, on a section of the Bombing and Gunnery Range of the new Alamogordo Army Air Field. The desolate area was called Jornado del Muerto, the "Journey of the Dead."

Politics determined the date. On May 8, Germany had surrendered. The war in Europe was over. The feared German atomic bomb had never been built.

On July 15, Harry Truman, president since Roosevelt's death, arrived in Soviet-occupied Potsdam, Germany, to meet major allies, England's Churchill and the Soviet Union's Stalin. A few months earlier, while he was still vice president, Truman had known nothing of the Manhattan Project. But now he intended to issue an ultimatum of surrender to Japan, whose armies were collapsing. American bombers were smashing and burning Japanese cities, while battleships pounded Japanese industries along the coast.

Unconditional surrender was unthinkable to the Japanese. They feared their emperor would be executed as a common war criminal. Their savage resistance and kamikaze attacks at the battle for Okinawa suggested that an American invasion of Japan's main islands could result in a quarter of a million American deaths.

Emperor Hirohito of Japan

Trinity site

Could the surrender ultimatum include a threat of total annihilation? President Truman needed to know if the atomic bomb worked.

Now the focus of attention rested in a flimsy metal shed perched atop a 100-foot (30-meter) "shot" tower at Ground Zero, the spot where the explosion would go off. Tangled in its firing cables, the "gadget" looked like a giant black pumpkin caught in the grip of a 64-armed relative of an octopus. At its core, surrounded by thick layers of explosives, was a baseball-sized ball of pure plutonium weighing only 13 pounds (6 kilograms). At dusk Donald Hornig, designer of the electronic detonator, plugged in the bomb. Later, at Oppy's request, Hornig returned to the shed to baby-sit. He read a book while gusts of wind rattled the shed, crackling lightning bolts stitched the sky, and thunder boomed.

Trinity steel tower, which was destroyed by the test blast.

Trinity, the first atomic bomb.

At 4:45 A.M., with storms moving off and clouds breaking up, the bosses agreed to fire at 5:30. The firing team unlocked and set the timing and sequence circuits, and they armed the safety switch. Then they retreated to a massive earth-and-concrete bunker almost 6 miles (10 kilometers) from the tower. General Groves joined other scientists at Base Camp, 4 miles (6.5 kilometers) further south. Fuchs and 90 other Los Alamos spectators were scattered atop a hill 17 miles (27 kilometers) northwest of Ground Zero.

Sam Allison called out the world's first nuclear countdown into a microphone, as warning flares blazed and sirens blared. Joe McKibben threw each of the last arming switches. At T minus 45 seconds, he flipped an ordinary toggle switch to start automatic timers. Don Hornig's hand hovered over an "abort" switch that could cut the firing circuits in an emergency. Oppy, staring straight ahead, gripped a post.

Time-lapsed sequence of the explosion.

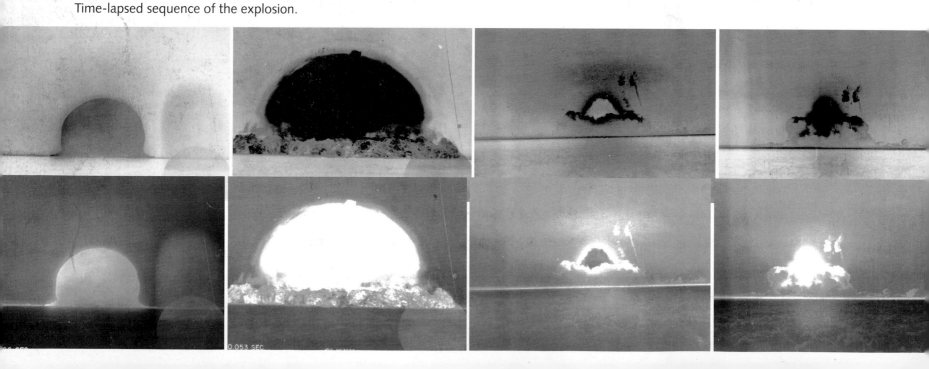

The crater
left by Trinity.

"Oppy" and General Groves

James B. Conant and Vannevar Bush, two of the scientists at Los Alamos, congratulate each other after the successful Trinity test.

Worried that he might be electrocuted by the microphone, Allison dropped it at T minus one second, screaming, "Now!" At precisely 5:29:45 A.M. Mountain War Time, the bomb exploded. A tremendous flash and brilliant flare lit the desert brighter than the noontime sun. The steel tower was totally vaporized, down to its concrete foundation stubs. Its atoms were ionized, torn apart by the nuclear energy released. A wave of searing heat washed over the observers.

Physicist Richard Feynman ducked. He looked up to see the dazzling white light change to yellow, then orange. Clouds formed and disappeared. A big ball of smoke, ripped with flashes of orange flame, started to rise from the desert floor.

The expanding fireball touched the desert, scooping out a broad, shallow saucer-shaped crater about a quarter mile (400 meters) across. It melted the sand for hundreds of yards around the tower. As it cooled, it hardened into a dull jade-green crust—a new atomic-age mineral later named Trinitite.

Lines from the sacred Hindu text Bhagavad Gita flashed through Oppy's mind: "I am become Death . . . the shatterer of worlds."

9

Enola Gay *Delivers "Little Boy"*

Enola Gay

Colonel Paul Tibbets

August 6, 1945

Colonel Paul Tibbets, commanding officer of the 509th Composite Group, attached to the 313th Bombardment Wing, 20th Air Force, felt his palms grow sweaty. He was gripping the control yoke of a modified B-29 Superfortress whose four engines were running with a deafening roar.

The plane, Number 82, shuddered against its brakes at the end of a long, chipped coral runway on tiny Tinian, one of the Mariana Islands in the South Pacific. From Tinian and nearby Guam and Saipan, hundreds of B-29s had massed for strikes against Japan, 1,400 miles (2,300 kilometers) away. This time, only seven were making the trip, and only the *Enola Gay* was carrying a bomb.

Two days earlier General Curtis LeMay, Chief of Staff to General Carl Spaatz, head of Strategic Air Forces, Pacific, had arrived on Tinian to personally deliver the order for Special Bombing Mission Number 13.

Navy Captain William "Deke" Parsons, head of the Ordnance Division at Los Alamos, briefed the air crews about the Manhattan Project. He had wanted to show a film of the Trinity test, but there were projector problems.

Captain "Deke" Parsons

"Little Boy"

The ground grew of *Enola Gay.*

Parsons added his own eyewitness description to still pictures of the test. There was a shocked silence when he said that this one bomb was expected to knock out almost everything within a 3-mile (5-kilometer) area. He finished by sketching a large mushroom-shaped cloud on the blackboard.

On August 5, Tibbets had watched as the nuclear bomb "Little Boy" was hoisted into *Enola Gay's* bomb bay. He found the name curious, because "Little Boy" was a giant compared to any bomb he had ever dropped. Over 10 feet (3 meters) long and almost 30 inches (75 centimeters) across, it weighed close to 5 tons (4.5 tonnes). It seemed incredible to Tibbets that this single bomb, however huge, should have the explosive force of 20,000 tons (18,000 tonnes) of TNT—the explosive power of 200,000 of the sort of bombs dropped on Europe and Africa during the war.

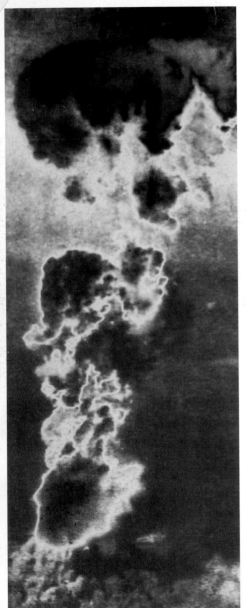

Tibbets looked at his watch. It was 2:45 A.M. The bomb, the crew, and now the plane were ready. Tibbets released the brakes. Enola Gay crawled into the moonless sky. Her destination: Hiroshima, Japan.

The decision to drop the bomb on this Japanese city bustling with civilians had been difficult to make. President Truman had hoped for a purely military target. Hiroshima was a major port and a military head-quarters, but thousands of civilian deaths would be unavoidable. Some advisers believed, however, that bombing an urban area might cripple the fighting will of the Japanese people. Large areas of many Japanese cities, including Tokyo, had already been heavily destroyed by B-29 fire-bomb attacks. Hiroshima was chosen because it was relatively undamaged, and the effects of the new bomb could be measured. Visual bombing—not radar—would be used, so photographs could be taken of the damage.

"Little Boy" was a much simpler nuclear bomb than the "Fat Man" model tested at Trinity site. The scientists considered its simple "gun-barrel" design so reliable that it had never been tested. Indeed, a test was out of the question. "Little Boy" had used all of the purified U^{235} produced to date.

To sift enough U^{235} for another "Little Boy" would require several months. On the other hand, enough plutonium was flowing from Hanford to have one "Fat Man" bomb ready along with "Little Boy." So "Little Boy" turned out to be unique—there was never another bomb like it.

The mushroom cloud rising above Hiroshima when "Little Boy" exploded.

Leo Szilard, at Met Lab in Chicago, who had kick-started atomic bomb research in 1939, now was trying to stop the use of the bomb. The threat of a German bomb was over. He gathered 88 signatures on a petition to President Truman opposing the bomb's use against Japan. He had copies circulated in Chicago and at Oak Ridge. Oppy quashed the petition at Los Alamos.

General Groves got wind of the petition. He ordered his own poll of the Met Lab scientists. Only 15 percent wanted the bomb used "in the most effective military manner." The largest segment, 46 percent, voted for a vague "military demonstration in Japan to be followed by a new opportunity for surrender before full use of the weapon is employed." Somehow, the figures were manipulated so that they suggested 87 percent of Met Lab scientists *favored* some sort of military use!

In any event, Groves sat on Szilard's petition and the poll until August 1. Then he had them filed away. Truman never saw them.

The Japanese military, determined to fight on, ignored the Potsdam Declaration's threat of "prompt and utter destruction." Groves drafted the orders to be issued to General Carl Spaatz, commander of air forces in the Pacific. They were approved by Army Chief of Staff George C. Marshall, Secretary of War Stimson, and President Truman. The political and military momentum was unstoppable. Atomic bombs would be dropped on Japan.

Ten miles (16 kilometers) from Hiroshima, bombardier Major Tom Ferebee spotted the target, a peculiar T-shaped bridge at the junction of the Honkawa and Motoyasu rivers, near downtown.

At precisely 8:15:17 A.M. Hiroshima time, "Little Boy" tumbled out of *Enola Gay*'s bomb bay. Tibbets threw the plane into a steep diving turn, in order to escape. After 45 seconds of bomb flight the flash came. More than the momentary blinding light, Tibbets remembered feeling a distinct taste of lead on his tongue. Apparently the radiation from the bomb's burst struck the fillings of his teeth and caused a chemical reaction. Two shock waves struck the plane—one directly from the blast, the other reflected off the ground.

Already a giant, purple-streaked mushroom cloud had risen 3 miles (5 kilometers) higher than the 6-mile (10-kilometers) altitude of the plane and was still boiling upward. Hiroshima had disappeared under a thick, churning foam of flames and smoke as a hurricane of fire ravaged the city. Shock and horror swept over the crew.

Co-pilot Richard Lewis exclaimed, "My God, what have we done?"

Secretary of War Henry L. Stimson and Secretary of State Jimmy Byrnes

Army Chief of Staff George C. Marshall

10

Pika-Don

After a fall of 6 miles (10 kilometers), "Little Boy" missed the T-shaped Aioi Bridge in Hiroshima by less than 300 yards (275 meters). It exploded roughly 2,000 feet (600 meters) directly above the courtyard to Dr. Kaoru Shima's small private hospital, with a power equal to 15,000 tons (13,600 tonnes) of TNT. The stone columns of the hospital building were driven several feet (about one meter) straight down into the ground. Most of the building and all the patients were instantly atomized.

Perhaps 80,000 people were killed instantly. The death toll would reach 140,000—roughly half the population.

Three days later, on August 9, "Fat Man"—dropped miles away from its original target because of the cloud cover—fell in the narrow, heavily industrialized Urakami Valley northwest of downtown Nagasaki. It exploded roughly 1,600 feet (500 meters) above Japan's largest Roman Catholic cathedral, with a force of 22,000 tons (20,000 tonnes) of TNT. The Urakami Cathedral, with two Japanese Roman Catholic priests and perhaps fifty people waiting to say confession, instantly disintegrated.

The blast was boxed in by the river valley; deaths in Nagasaki were somewhat fewer than in Hiroshima. About 40,000 died instantly, 70,000 by the end of 1945.

Both cities were devastated. For over a mile (nearly 2 kilometers) in every direction, almost all buildings were demolished. The few earthquake-proof concrete structures were heavily damaged and burned. Fires raged for days.

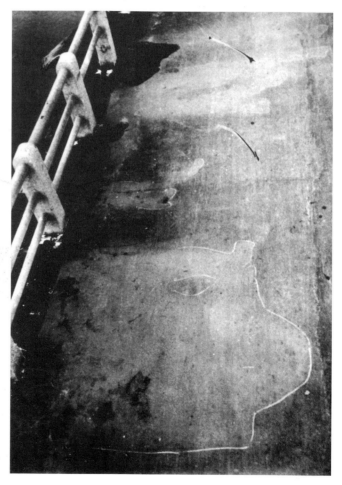

The imprint iof a man pulling a cart on unburned asphalt in Hiroshima.

A lone bicyclist among the twisted remains of electrical poles.

A street two miles from the center of the explosion in Hiroshima, two hours after the blast.

A Japanese soldier looks at the skeleton of a building in Hiroshima.

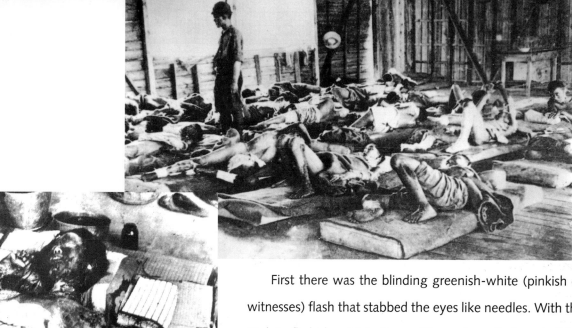

A Japanese soldier watches the injured and dying in a Hiroshima makeshift hospital.

A seriously burned victim.

First there was the blinding greenish-white (pinkish or orange or rainbow-hued, according to different witnesses) flash that stabbed the eyes like needles. With the flash of light came searing waves of radiant heat. Birds in flight burst into flame. Tile roofs melted; asphalt boiled; telephone poles and railroad ties ignited.

Exposed skin was instantly charred and blistered by the burning rays. The blast that followed peeled the skin loose, leaving it dangling from red and bleeding arms and legs like tattered rags. Dark patterns on clothes were branded into the flesh beneath.

The hundreds of fires and furious updraft into the mushroom cloud combined at Hiroshima to produce a hurricane of flame, a "fire storm," that incinerated everything within miles. People surged toward Hiroshima's several rivers to escape the flames and to try to ease the pain of their burns. Soon the rivers were clogged with floating corpses.

After the blinding flash and the blazing heat, the nuclear fist pounded the cities flat. The blast wave started at ten times the speed of sound, gradually slowing as it smashed outward through the cities. Over two-thirds of Hiroshima's buildings were demolished. Flying glass slivers from shattered windows became lethal daggers.

In Nagasaki, the cathedral bell tower was twisted into a mass of tangled iron. Railroad tracks, trestles, and the steel-framed Mitsubishi arms factories crumpled away from the blast. Their warped iron skeletons sagged. The steel towers of power lines were twisted like licorice.

Besides its blowtorching tongues of flame, beyond its crushing tons of supersonic shock waves, the bomb unleashed a gale of deadly rays. High-energy neutrons, gamma rays, and X rays assaulted even those behind concrete walls.

Huge dark clouds spread out in the sky, and black rain began to fall. The thick, muddy drops, cold and stinging, coated injured bodies with black grit: the first lethal radioactive "fallout."

- "Radiation sickness" symptoms showed up only days after the bombing, but the internal damage could take terrible weeks or months to prove fatal. Early signs were purplish-brown spots like bruises, about the size of a dime, appearing all over the body. Appetites failed. Hair fell out. Victims bled from their gums, vomited, and suffered bloody diarrhea. Blood tests revealed that their levels of infection-fighting white blood cells were dangerously low. As their bodies lost the battle with the massive radiation damage, people slowly grew weaker, collapsed, and died.

Survivors of the bombings were left scarred, marked by hideous rubbery scar tissue and invisible damage from radiation. Studies show that cancer—particularly leukemia—struck survivors more often than would be expected.

Many surviving women who were pregnant when exposed to the bomb's radiation had miscarriages or stillbirths. Depending on the mothers' distance from the blast, some babies were born physically healthy but severely mentally retarded. There were no cases, however, of the monstrous "mutants" so often featured in science fiction.

The survivors coined a word to describe the horrible new weapon. It combined the sounds of crackling lightning with the deafening clap of thunder: Pika-Don—"flash-bang" or perhaps "crack-boom."

On August 15, Japan surrendered. World War II was over at last.

A drawing by a bomb survivor, showing survivors crossing the Aioi Bridge and the corpses clogging the river.

11

1,000 Paper Cranes

Los Alamos receiving an award from the Army and the Navy.

Victory celebrations broke out at all Manhattan Project laboratories as Groves released the story of the atomic bomb to newspapers and radio. At Los Alamos, the party was a flop. Oppy dropped by only briefly to find one group leader vomiting in the bushes outside. The reaction had begun.

Leo Szilard was horrified to hear the news of Hiroshima but relieved that the secret was out. Now the future of nuclear weapons could be openly debated. Many Manhattan Project scientists had deep, painful feelings of responsibility for the terrible weapon. Some stopped working on military weapons. Others left the field of physics entirely.

A large group of the scientists sat down to consider seriously what should be done with this monster they had made. The Association of Los Alamos Scientists, formed to educate the public about atomic energy and to promote international control of nuclear weapons, soon joined with organizations at other Manhattan Project labs to form the Federation of American Scientists.

Its vigorous political efforts led to the creation of a completely civilian Atomic Energy Commission and generated a campaign for international agreements to regulate or ban nuclear weapons.

Many researchers left Los Alamos soon after the war ended. Others felt that the entire lab should be closed down. Some, however, stayed to design smaller, more efficient atomic fission weapons. A few, led by Edward Teller, continued development of the "Super," a thermonuclear hydrogen bomb of vast power.

February 1955

One day a Japanese girl named Sadako Sasaki collapsed while running at school. Her father was called. He took her to the Hiroshima Red Cross Hospital. After X rays, blood tests, and consultations with several doctors, Sadako and her family were told the grim news. Sadako had leukemia, a cancer of the lymph system and bone marrow, where the body makes new blood cells.

Leukemia prevents the white blood cells—the body's main defense against infection—from doing their job properly. The disease also interferes with the normal production of oxygen-carrying red blood cells and the platelet cells that make blood clot. (In Sadako's time, only a few of every hundred leukemia patients survived. Today, with modern drug treatment, a child with leukemia has better than two-to-one odds of a normal lifespan.)

As a two-year-old, Sadako had survived the atomic blast and the hurricane of fire without a scratch. Nevertheless, nuclear radiation had damaged critical parts of her rapidly growing body. The damaged cells hid for ten years as she grew up. Now, suddenly, her body could not manufacture its own blood properly.

From her hospital bed, Sadako bravely kept up with her schoolwork, laughing and singing with her visiting classmates. She hoped with all her heart that she would get well and be able to make the track team.

At the hospital her first visitor was her best friend, Chizuko, who reminded her of the Japanese legend of the crane: A crane can live 1,000 years. Anyone who made 1,000 folded-paper cranes would be granted her dearest wish.

Taking a square of gold-colored paper, Chizuko used the ancient Japanese art of paper folding called origami to fashion a crane. She handed it to Sadako. When Sadako held the golden bird, she found the courage to face her illness.

The Children's Memorial in Peace Park at Hiroshima.

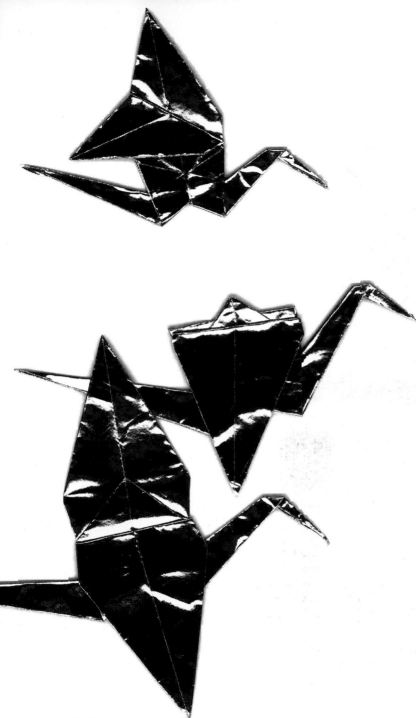

Sadako decided to fold 1,000 paper cranes. For weeks, as she battled the disease, she folded cranes. Her brother Masahiro strung her flock of hundreds of colorful cranes from her hospital-room ceiling.

On October 25 she died, having folded 644 paper cranes. Her school friends folded another 356. All 1,000 were placed in Sadako's coffin.

Sadako's friends vowed that no more innocent children would die in an uncaring world that wanted to forget the horror of the atomic bomb. They began a campaign to raise money for a children's monument to be built in Hiroshima's Peace Park, near where "Little Boy" had exploded. It would be a memorial to Sadako and to all young people who had suffered from the atomic bombing.

1958

Their dream came true.

Atop a tall, rounded granite pedestal symbolizing the mountain of paradise, stands a statue of Sadako. In her outstretched arms she holds a wire frame of a giant golden crane. Around the base of the monument are hundreds of paper chains, each strung with 1,000 cranes.

Today, origami cranes are sent to Hiroshima not only from the rest of Japan but from all over the world. Each year on the anniversary of the bombing, the Folded Crane Club holds a special service. Carrying photographs, framed in black ribbon, of children who died because of the atomic bomb, they drape new chains of paper cranes around the pedestal. They renew their simple plea to the world, which is inscribed on the monument:

This is our cry,

this is our prayer:

peace in the world.

The Hiroshima Memorial Cenotaph, which contains the list of names of
those who died when the atomic bomb was dropped on Hiroshima, has this
written on it: "Repose ye in peace, for the error shall never be repeated."

Index

Text copyright © 1995 Tom Seddon.

All rights reserved. No part of this book may be reproduced by any mechanical, photographic, or electronic process, or in the form of a phonographic recording, nor may it be stored in a retrieval system, transmitted, or otherwise copied for public or private use, without written permission from the publisher.

Book design by Maria Epes.

Scientific American Books for Young Readers is an imprint of W. H. Freeman and Company, 41 Madison Avenue, New York, NY 10010.

Library of Congress Catologing-in-Publication Data

Seddon, Tom.
    Atom bomb / Tom Seddon.
    Includes index.
Summary: Discusses the use of the atomic bomb on Hiroshima and Nagasaki, from the scientific beginnings to the tragic aftermath.
        ISBN 0-7167-6582-9 (Hardcover)
1. Hiroshima-shi (Japan)—History—Bombardment, 1945—Juvenile literature. 2. Nagasaki-shi (Japan)—History—Bombardment, 1945—Juvenile literature. 3. Atomic bomb—History—Juvenile literature. [1. Hiroshima-shi (Japan)—History—Bombardment, 1945. 2. Nagasaki-shi (Japan) —History—Bombardment, 1945. 3. Atomic bomb—History.] I. Title.
D767.25.H6S35   1995
940.54′25—dc20

                                95-18871

                            CIP

                            AC

Printed in the United States of America.
10 9 8 7 6 5 4 3 2 1

Photo Credits

Front Cover
Trinity blast: Rene Burri/Magnum; Enrico Fermi: Archive Photos
Back Cover (from left to right)
H. G. Wells, the British writer whose 1914 novel, *The World Set Free,* predicted the development of atomic bombs and atomic war: Culver Pictures; Leo Szilard: Argonne National Laboratory; a meeting of wartime scientists in 1940 (Ernest Lawrence, Arthur Compton, Vannevar Bush, James B. Conant, Karl Compton, and Alfred Loomis): Lawrence Berkeley Laboratory; President Harry S. Truman: Archive Photos; the crew of the Enola Gay (Major Thomas Ferebee, Colonel Paul Tibbets, Captain Theodore Van Kirk, and Captain Robert Lewis): Culver Pictures
Introduction
p. 1: (background and foreground) Archive Photos; p. 2: (background left and right) Archive Photos, (foreground) UPI/Bettmann Newsphotos; p. 3: (left and right) Archive Photos; p. 4: (left) Archive Photos, (right) Asahi Shimbun; p. 5: (left, center, and right) Asahi Shimbun
Chapter 1
p. 6: Argonne National Laboratory; p. 7: (top) Culver Pictures, (bottom) AIP Emilio Segrè Visual Archives, courtesy Otto Hahn and Lawrence Badash; p. 8: (top) Nobel Foundation, courtesy AIP Emilio Segrè Visual Archives, (center) Culver Pictures, (bottom) University of Chicago, courtesy AIP Emilio Segrè Visual Archives; p. 9: (top left) Otto Hahn, *A Scientific Autobiography,* New York, C. Scribner's Sons, 1966, courtesy AIP Emilio Segrè Visual Archives, (center left) AIP Emilio Segrè Visual Archives, Wheeler Collection, (right) Archive Photos/Popperophoto; p. 10: (top left) AIP Emilio Segrè Visual Archives, (both headlines) copyright 1939 by The New York Times Company, reprinted by permission
Chapter 2
p. 11: Argonne National Laboratory; p. 12: (top) Argonne National Laboratory, (center) Argonne National Laboratory, (bottom) Culver Pictures
Chapter 3
p. 13: Culver Pictures; p. 14: Culver Pictures; p. 15: Culver Pictures; p. 16: (top) Lawrence Berkeley Laboratory, (bottom) Martin Marietta
Chapter 4
p. 17: Argonne National Laboratory; p. 18: Argonne National Laboratory; p. 19: Culver Pictures
Chapter 5
p. 20: National Archives; p. 21: National Archives
Chapter 6
p. 22: (left) Los Alamos National Laboratory, (right) Archive Photos; p. 23: Los Alamos National Laboratory; p. 24: Los Alamos National Laboratory; p. 25: Los Alamos National Laboratory; pp. 26–27: all from Los Alamos National Laboratory
Chapter 7
p. 28: Archive Photos; p. 29: Archive Photos
Chapter 8
p. 30: Culver Pictures; p. 31: (left and right) Los Alamos National Laboratory; p. 32: (top) Rene Burri/Magnum, (bottom sequence) Los Alamos National Laboratory; p. 33: (top left) Rene Burri/Magnum, (top right) Archive Photos, (bottom right) The MIT Museum
Chapter 9
p. 34: (left and right) U.S. Air Force Photo Collection, courtesy the National Air and Space Museum, Smithsonian Institution; p. 35: (top left) Los Alamos National Laboratory, (top right) Archive Photos, (bottom) U.S. Air Force Photo Collection, courtesy the National Air and Space Museum, Smithsonian Institution; p. 36: (left and right) Archive Photos; p. 37: (top) Archive Photos, (bottom) Clemson University
Chapter 10
p. 38: Hiroshima Peace Culture Foundation; p. 39: (top left) Archive Photos, (top right) Culver Pictures, (bottom) UPI/Bettmann Newsphotos; p. 40–41: (top and left) Hiroshima Peace Culture Foundation
Chapter 11
p. 42: Los Alamos National Laboratory; p. 43: Archive Photos; p. 44: Peter Gave; p. 45: Archive Photos